Rambles In Northern India...

Francesca Henrietta Wilson

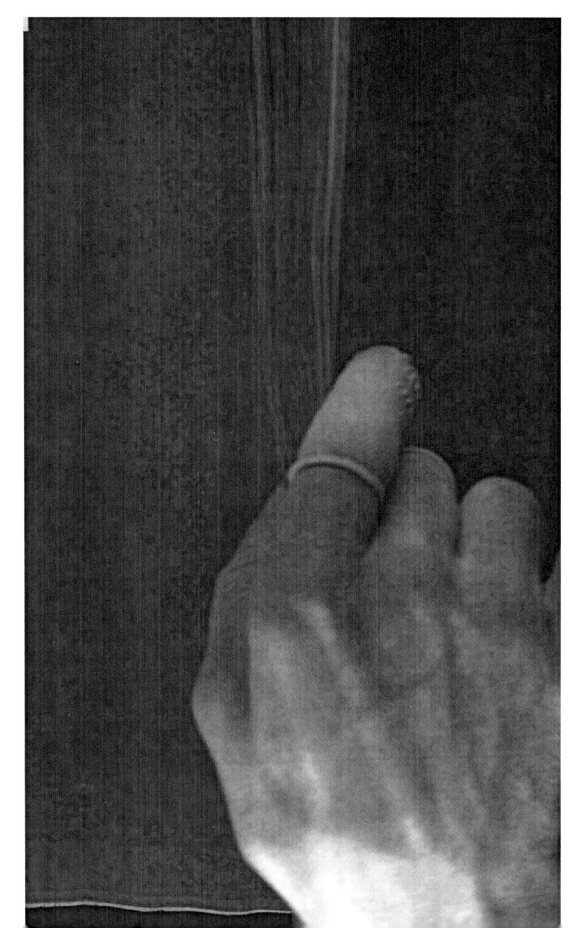

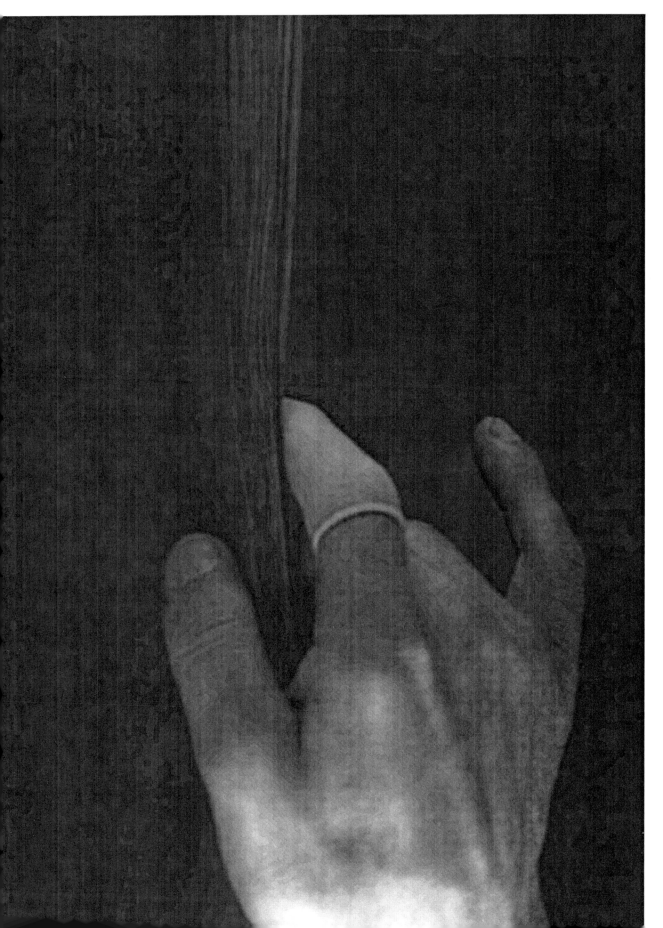

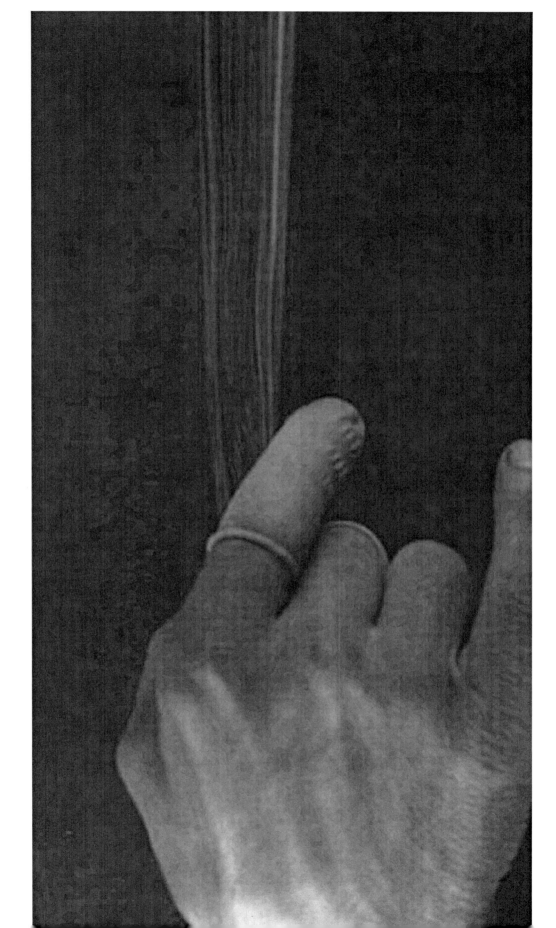

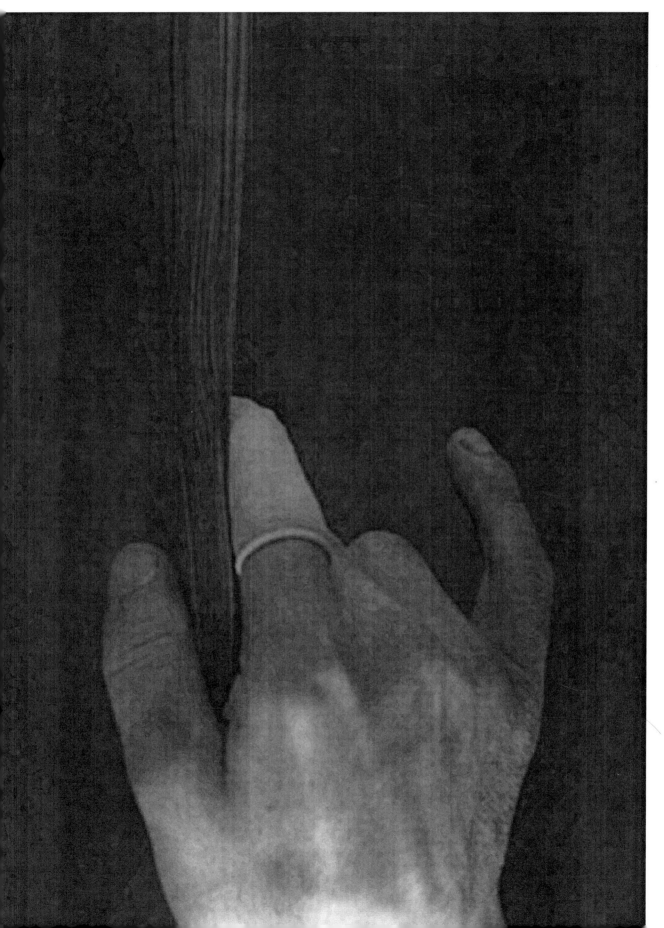

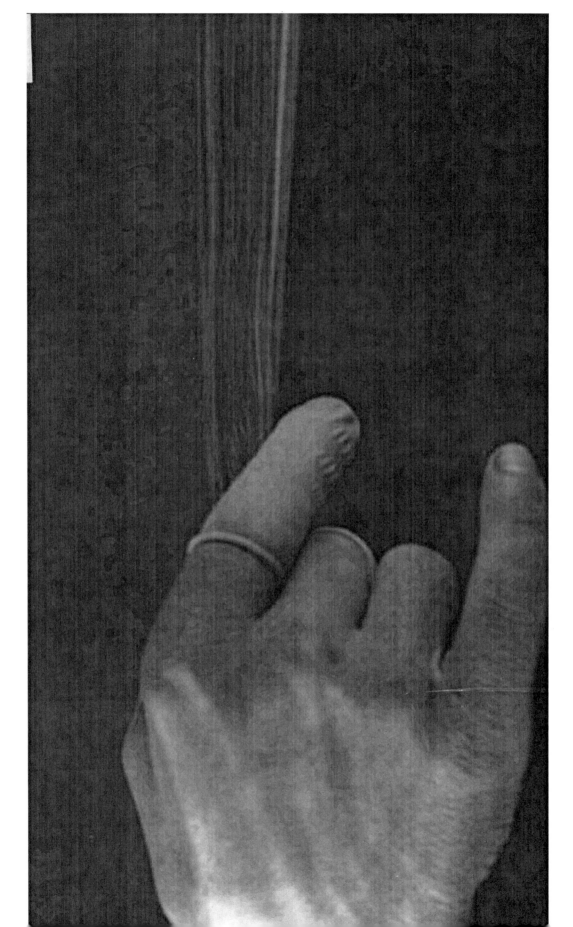

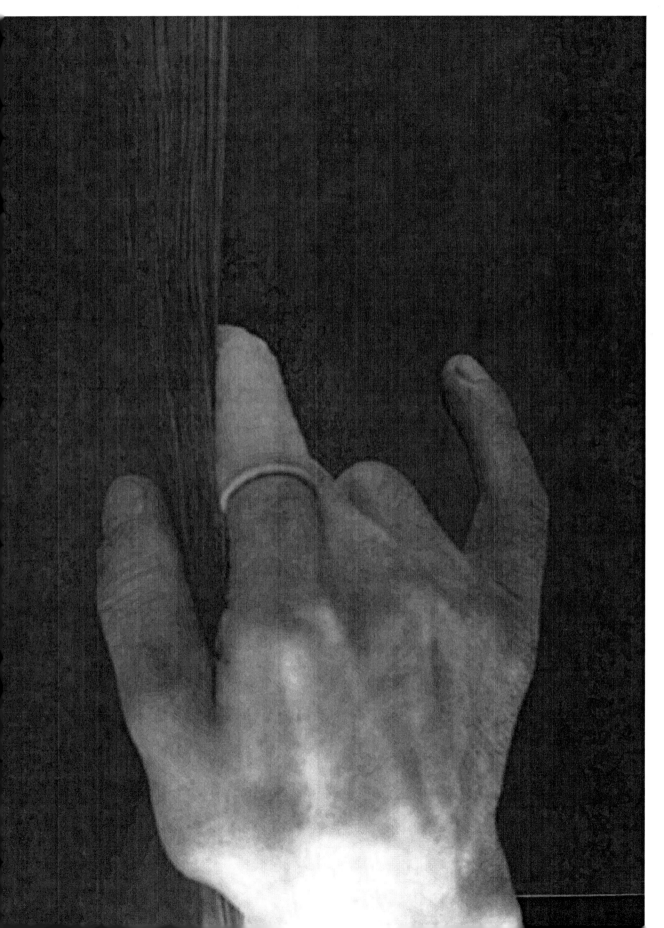

RAMBLES IN NORTHERN INDIA.

.

.

RAMBLES IN NORTHERN INDIA.

WITH INCIDENTS AND DESCRIPTIONS

OF MANY SCENES OF THE

MUTINY,

INCLUDING AGRA, DELHI, LUCKNOW, CAWNPORE,

ALLAHABAD, ETC.

WITH TWELVE LARGE PHOTOGRAPHIC VIEWS,

BY FRANCESCA H. WILSON,

AUTHOR OF " TRUTH BETTER THAN FICTION," ETC.

LONDON:

SAMPSON LOW, MARSTON, LOW, AND SEARLE,

CROWN BUILDINGS, 188, FLEET STREET.

1876.

CHISWICK PRESS :—PRINTED BY WHITTINGHAM AND WILKINS,
TOOKS COURT, CHANCERY LANE.

PREFACE.

THE incidents narrated in this volume are, I believe, perfectly authentic, my information having been derived from entirely reliable sources; and the photographs representing some of the scenes described have all been carefully selected, as being those that most truthfully portray their interesting and beautiful subjects.

FRANCESCA H. WILSON.

LONDON, *October*, 1875.

LIST OF PHOTOGRAPHS.

CONTENTS.

RAMBLES IN NORTHERN INDIA.

CHAPTER I.

My First Visit to the Himalayas.

"MY first visit to the Himalayas!" What an amount of griffinage does this little sentence express!—griffinage [1] which places one's first year in India completely in the shade. After a residence of some months at Simla (the seat of the Supreme Government of India during the hot season) one can afford to laugh at early experiences of mountain life; nevertheless,

---

[1] During a man's first year in India he is always styled a griffin, or griff, denoting inexperience, answering to the "freshman" of the Universities.

nothing short of an entire season can thoroughly initiate any one into the mysteries and peculiarities of existence in the Himalayas.

The town of Kalka lies on high ground at the foot of the mountains; it contains several inferior hotels, in which people seldom remain longer than is absolutely necessary to secure a sufficient number of janpans, coolies, ponies, and mules for the ascent. Gentlemen very frequently ride, while ladies and children are generally carried on the shoulders of coolies, seated in a sort of sedan chair called a janpan. The first thing that astonished me, on starting in a painfully rickety one, was, that the janpanees kept step as determinedly as any well-drilled body of soldiers. The effect of this may easily be imagined! In vain I screamed to them " Barabur challo! hillao mut!" (Go properly, don't shake); they took no notice, and only shook me worse than ever; so, at last, finding I was getting tired and hoarse without any benefit accruing therefrom, I ceased my cries in blank despair. I, who had been accustomed to the broad, well-made, and well-protected road up to Ootacamund in the Neilgherries, now discovered that I had a worse trial to bear than merely being badly shaken. Ere I had fairly left Kalka, I found myself ascending one of the steepest, narrowest, stoniest, and most dizzying roads I ever had the bad luck to travel on. They call it the old road to Simla, which I in ignorance, griffin as I was, chose in preference to the fine new road, the latter being longer; but, even now, it is the only road to the stations of Kussowlee and Sebattoo. Besides being frightfully narrow in parts, the turns are so sharp that one's janpan literally hangs over the precipice as the corner is being turned; there is not the smallest protection, so that, if a false step were made at this particular moment, a fearful accident must occur; and, while making the descent from Kussowlee, before the ascent to Sebattoo is commenced, one is swung round these turns in the most alarming manner, as the coolies race down as fast as their feet can carry them. To those who

are ill, or nervous, and to such as are afflicted with
weak heads, no words can describe the miseries
endured, because they cannot be cured, during this
journey up the mountains, which usually occupies
four days. The first resting place is Kussowlee,
which is higher than any point in Simla, being between 8,550 and 9,000 feet above the level of the
sea. The scenery is magnificent, and Simla itself
with its highest mountain, Jakko, are pretty objects
in the far distance.

One deplorable sign of my griffinage as to Himalayan ways was my failing to provide myself and
family with bedding. Being used to the comfortably
furnished Dâk Bungalows or Rest Houses in the
Madras Presidency, Central Provinces, &c., I never
dreamed of preparing mattresses, razaies (quilted
counterpanes), &c., for the journey; and after all,
even had I known that northern Indian Dâk Bungalows were destitute of these comforts, so necessary in
a cold climate, I could not have brought a sufficient
supply for so large a party without considerable

expense, as the East Indian Railway Company, charge for every bundle, basket, &c. It was, however, a cold, comfortless experience, this sleeping on a bare cot, and especially so when the tapes were sufficiently loose to admit of a child of eight years finding herself during the night, on the floor, under the bed! I may as well mention that broad tape, two or three inches wide, is frequently used for bedsteads in India instead of boards or canvas.

On reaching Boileau-Gunj—the entrance to Simla, I was overjoyed when I caught sight of the railings, which extend all along the Mall. " There's an end to unprotected *Khuds*" (precipices), said I, fondly imagining that all the roads in Simla were similarly guarded; but I was soon undeceived, and, horror of horrors! the very road, facetiously named "the Upper Mall," leading up to my future domicile, and not wider in several places than four and a half and five feet, was wholly innocent of either wall, or railing, except, indeed, in one or two spots where they are apparently least needed! It costs a mint of money to keep up even the present meagre amount of fencing, as, during the winter, in spite of the police, the railings are largely appropriated for fuel. The Mall, which extends for several miles right through Simla, is a fairly broad good road; this is the fashionable ride, and no portion of it is uncomfortably steep; but some of the less frequented roads are very bad indeed; and it is a wonder how people can become accustomed to them—which in an incredibly short time they do; I very soon ventured fearlessly on paths that at one time appeared to me wholly impracticable. However, I must confess that during the first stages of griffinage one's impulse is, having reached one's destination, to stay there; particularly if your house happens to be situated near the summit of the highest mountain in the place, and especially if condemned to take your "*howa khana*" (airing) in a janpan; unless, indeed, you can succeed in teaching your instruments of torture—the janpances—to adopt the Madras shuffle.

I must here explain that Madras bearers rarely shake sufficiently to annoy the person they are carrying, owing to their never keeping step; whereas the effect produced by the Hill janpanee's regularity of step is both distressing and ridiculous in the extreme.

We were previously warned that the servants here, as in most Hill stations, were untrustworthy; so fortunately brought some of our own, and consequently suffered less than our neighbours, who, whether they knew it or not, had to pay heavily for every thing they purchased, owing to the *dustoori* (commission) expected by the servants, who ply quite a thriving trade in this way. They, one and all, endeavour to impose as much as possible—easily discovering that you are a griff as to wages, prices, *kam* (work), &c., in short, to everything Himalayan. The very objectionable habit of *hubble-bubbling* (hookah-smoking) is a perfect infliction; and the owners of unaccustomed Madras olfactories are forced to decline the honour of being served by hookah-smoking domestics. Nearly every one keeps a certain number of janpanees, who not only carry out the janpan if required, but go daily to the jungles in the interior, some five miles distant, and cut and fetch wood, which, besides charcoal, is the only kind of fuel used.

The monsoon or rainy season in Simla is sadly trying to one's patience. It is extremely aggravating to know that but for perpetual clouds the most glorious scenery would be visible: the clouds very often enter houses, and, unless doors and windows are quickly closed, everything is rendered moist, and too often ruined in consequence. To compensate for these disadvantages, we were often rewarded by the most beautiful sights and changes that it is possible to imagine; nay, I despair of any description being adequate to convey a correct idea of these rapidly fleeting and most glorious scenes.

One instant we were enveloped in dense black clouds; suddenly a gap in them appeared, and, though all above and around was dark, the valley, upwards of

2,000 feet below, and the base of the opposite mountains were illuminated by brilliant dazzling sun-light, made all the more unearthly in its resplendence by the surrounding obscurity.

The stream at the foot of the mountains, the rocks, ferns, grass, shrubs, cedars, &c., were arrayed in lovely and ever-varying tints; while the summit of the mountains on which they grow were hidden by dense clouds as white as snow.

Very frequently at sunset a marvellous scene presented itself: the clouds below us on the Simla side suddenly became exquisitely tinted by the setting sun; and, in far less time than I can write it, they rolled themselves up, and dispersed; the mountains, thirteen ranges of which were visible, the houses, and other objects in Simla—1,000 feet below—came out, one by one, as if in a dissolving view, only to disappear as rapidly as they appeared. As the sun sank lower and lower, the rays through the clouds became more and more beautiful; and the room seemed illuminated by the softest moonlight, so unlike the " greater light " did it appear. Such scenes as these are not enjoyed except by those who live at a great height, but, when once seen, make the deepest impression on every thoughtful mind. The clouds at times dispersed at sunset sufficiently to give us a splendid view of the plains, when the colour of the water, trees, &c., were distinctly visible ; and when the great river Sutlej, then swollen by the rains, could be traced for many miles, lit up like molten gold by the setting sun, until it was lost to sight on the far-off horizon. Sometimes, after a heavier shower than usual, the atmosphere would clear, and the sun come forth shedding his radiance in richest hues on mountain and vale. One peak would have the appearance of being clothed in the softest green velvet, another in dark purple, and another in grey, and all the colours were intensified by the fleecy clouds which hung about the mountain tops.

The pines at Simla are very beautiful, as also are the American oaks, whose trunks are generally covered with ferns. The latter abound, and also wild flowers, among which the snake plant, red and white lilies, orchids, varied and handsome dahlias are during the rainy season most worthy of notice; but, almost daily then, some new and lovely specimen of Himalayan flora springs up.

Large and finely flavoured strawberries, very good golden plums, and as nice apples as I ever tasted in England are to be had in Simla. Excellent vegetables are also procurable by employing a *Mallie* or gardener to supply them at the cost of five rupees (ten shillings) a month. These are brought from Sahiri; and, notwithstanding the distance they have to travel, are wonderfully fresh when they arrive. All "Europe articles," owing to their carriage up the mountains, are very expensive, as also fowls, beef, and eggs; potatoes, being extraordinarily abundant, are cheap.

Simla is, during the monsoon, frequently visited by terrific storms of thunder and lightning; some of which last season were attended with fatal results;

however, as a rule, Simla is peculiarly still and wind-less, and the climbers who on foot ascend some of the steep hills in and around the place are, to their infinite discomfort, obliged to acknowledge that it is certainly not without truth that Simla is called "the stillest place in India."

CHAPTER II.

Umritsur.

MY first visit to the Himalayas is now a thing of the past; all that is left to me are memories, mostly pleasant ones, and photographs, that at the best convey but a poor idea of scenery which owes half its beauty to the wondrous shades and marvellous tints that are so peculiarly Himalayan. Before leaving Simla, and at the conclusion of the rainy season, we were enabled to take a short trip into the interior, and our only regret was that want of time prevented a longer stay amidst scenery which throws that of Simla, beautiful as it is, into the shade. The road a short distance from Simla is cut right through a mountain, and, this being the only tunnel in that part of the

Himalayas, is an object of interest.   Some miles further on, the road narrows considerably, and becomes more and more beautiful ; one requires, however, strong nerve to endure some of the sharp precipitous turns in the path, which, though every minute discovering new beauties to astonished eyes, yet make one feel the reverse of safe as one winds round the corner, the janpanees treading on the edge of an awful precipice all through the process.

The view of the snowy range, which towers above the nearer mountains upwards of 100 miles away, the exquisite wild flowers, ferns of every sort, &c., are never to be forgotten; and the further you advance into the interior the grander and more magnificent is the scenery.   One must expect every now and then to meet with obstacles in the path.   In one or two places, the road was almost entirely washed away by the late rains ; there was, however, just room for a man's feet with difficulty to pass, but in another spot every vestige of a road had utterly disappeared, and the only way in which the gap could possibly be crossed, was over the trunk of a tree which spanned the chasm.

Before quitting the subject of the Himalayas, I must say a word in praise of that extraordinary piece of engineering—the new road from Kalka to Simla. It will be remembered that one of the fruits of my griffinage, when first I ascended the mountains, was the choosing the old in preference to the new road. I have now had experience of both routes, and consider this new broad road a marvel of the age; it is cut out of the sides of the mountains, and is supported in numerous places by massive walls. The descent was so gradual, that, though during the last march of fifteen miles we descended over 7,000 feet, one could hardly imagine that in some parts there was any hill at all, or, if so, there was absolutely nothing approaching a steep bit. It is only when looking back at the heights above that the tremendous descent is apparent, and even then the plains are reached ere one at all realizes their vicinity. The distance from the foot of the Himalayas to Simla is fifty-nine miles, which can be easily accomplished in twelve hours by Tonga Dâk.[1]

Kalka, though in the plains, lies on high ground, the long inclined plane thence extends nearly half-way to Umballa, a distance of thirty-eight miles— a most unpleasant road during the rains, as there are several broad unbridged rivers which can only be crossed in boats or on elephants.

Umballa is a very large fine station, but beyond a noble church, Paget's Park, and the Mall, there is nothing to see. The church is said to be the finest but one (that of Mean Meer) in India; the stained glass windows are magnificent, but very ugly punkahs do their utmost to spoil the effect of this otherwise beautiful building. Umritsur is one of the spots most worth seeing in the Punjaub; it is—as doubtless every one knows—the capital of the Sikhs, and as such is doubly interesting, and in many ways

---

[1] A Tonga Dâk consists of a covered spring cart, drawn by a pair of ponies, with a centre board that divides the two back from the two front seats, the travellers thus sitting back to back.

different to other large cities. It is here that the
great sight of the Punjaub is to be seen; I refer
to the golden Temple of Umritsur. It is so unique,
so unlike anything but itself, that nobody should
be within 200 miles of it, and not visit it. The
Temple rises out of the centre of a pretty tank,
or lake as it is called, the blue rippling waves of
which wash against the inlaid polished white marble
court-yard which surrounds the lake. The Temple
is connected with the same by a broad roadway
of similar marble, protected by a golden balustrade,
and golden lamps line the road on either side. The
lower half of the outside walls of the building are
elaborately carved white marble, the doors being solid
silver, and the windows golden; while the upper
half and the roof are a mass of gold, the ornamentation being numerous pretty minarets and a large
bell, all made, like the rest, of brass covered with
a thick plate of gold. The outside of the building is very striking, and the appearance is dazzling as it glistens in the brilliant sunlight, and

is reflected in the sparkling waters of the lake. The inside—and indeed the entire edifice—is, as I said before, unique; the flooring mosaic marble, the roof consisting of thousands of looking-glasses inlaid in the most beautiful golden work, interspersed with the richest scarlet and blue lacquer-work, is nowhere imitated, except in a temple in Lahore, where, however, the resemblance is but small; the latter being very inferior. There are several chambers off the centre one under the dome, which alternate in gold and silver work; and it is hard to decide which is most striking. However, with me, the golden chambers gained the preference. In both the lower and first stories of these chambers, there are priests continually employed; one to read out of the holy book belonging to the Temple, and the other to prevent even a fly from resting on the sacred pages. This he does by waving a long hair fly-flapper over the volume, sitting by the side of the priest, who reads in a droning, monotonous voice. The excessive greed displayed by the priests was both amusing and disgusting—every one expected to be feed, not excepting the men whose business it was to tie on the cloth shoes, which the police presented for our use on removal of our own shoes or boots. One must undergo this humiliating process, or one is not permitted to go down into the paved court surrounding the lake.

Umritsur is further celebrated for the produce of the genuine Indian shawls which are made there. We watched the workmen as they stitched in the most rapid manner, and can hardly wonder at the enormous price asked for, and fetched by, these shawls, seeing the tremendous labour entailed in their manufacture. I was disappointed with the Umritsur gardens, supposed to be the most beautiful in India. Throughout my travels, I hardly saw more ordinary gardens; they are pretty, but nothing particularly worthy of notice. The roads, on the contrary, struck me as being very fine, exceedingly broad, level, and extending for immense distances. The Fort, which bears the marks of many a fight, is an interesting old building, but it falls short, in both interest and beauty, of that of Lahore, where there is much to occupy one's attention. For the benefit of those who may be thinking of visiting Umritsur, I recommend the Railway Hotel ; cooking and attendance excellent, most civil, cleanly servants, and moderate charges being among the virtues of the place.

CHAPTER III.

LAHORE AND AGRA.

AHORE, the capital of the Punjaub, is reached after a short railway drive of thirty-two miles from Umritsur; it is at present the terminus of the Northern Railroad, but before long the line will be extended. In the Lahore Fort is the old Sikh armoury, which contains truly curious relics of bygone ages. There are, among other objects of interest, very ancient revolving guns, sixteen of them, four in a row, revolving in a square axle; there are also revolving matchlocks; curious swords, old Sikh colours, armour, &c., besides relics of the Mutiny of 1857. Opposite this building is the former palace of the king. It is

now but faded splendour — elaborate carving, gilt
work, &c., all suffering at the hands of the destroyer
—Time. The bathing apartments of the king and
queen must have been gorgeous in their day;
the doors, roof, &c., mother-o'-pearl inlaid in silver,
all now wearing a sad look of glory departed. From
the summit of the Summun Boorj, there is an extensive view of the surrounding country, and of
the city of Lahore and its station. The latter is
certainly a very fine one, and some of its public
buildings might well grace a Presidency town. The
most extraordinary are the two churches, formerly
mosques. The ingenuity displayed in the conversion
of one of these is remarkable; and the dome, which
is painted azure blue with golden stars, harmonizes
well with the rest of the interior. It is, moreover,
a strange and gratifying sight to see the cross reared
above the dome of what, from the outside, appears
to be merely a mosque. The tomb of Runjeet Singh,
situated outside the Fort in which he used to live,
is very pretty. The outside is plain white marble,

beautifully carved; the inside, as I before mentioned, is a faint imitation of the interior of the Golden Temple. On the tomb itself are little monuments to the memory of the seven wives and two butlers of the king, who, according to custom, were burnt to death on the funeral pyre of their Royal Master. The public gardens at Lahore are fine, with well-kept lawns, and ample room for driving about the inclosure. The gardens belonging to Government House are very pretty, and the *Chiryah Khana*, or place where birds are (though there are at present more beasts than birds there), is worthy of a visit, for the grounds are tastefully laid out, with water, &c., and the Lawrence Hall, the public rooms of the station, is a large and handsome block of buildings in the centre of the *Chiryah Khana* gardens. There are several hotels in Lahore, and the competition between the managers, who come to the Railway Station to meet the train, is beyond anything confusing and disagreeable. There is a deadly feud between the two new Victoria Hotels. The real original new Victoria is the one beneath the hill; I mention this for the benefit of travellers, to save them the inconvenience suffered by ourselves. The latter is most comfortable, food and attendance good, and manager most civil.

Mean Meer is situated about five or six miles from Lahore, and is about the most dreary, barren, miserable place I ever visited. The soil is sandy, resembling that of a desert, and of a reddish hue; while the absence of grass, and the scarcity of trees, give a forlorn appearance not easily imagined. The single object of interest is the church, which is considered the finest in all India. Why such a beautiful edifice should have been built in such a place no one knows, and it appears quite a pity it should have been so. Every window is coloured, and most of the subjects are well chosen and very effective.

I think, of all the places in the plains of Upper India, I should best like to live in Agra. It is such an interesting spot, without the dilapidated appear-

ance of many of the scenes of the struggle of 1857. The great sight, every one knows, is the Taj Mahal. I had read of it, had seen models and photographs of it, but had not the faintest idea of its extraordinary beauty till I saw the reality. It is, I believe, the beautiful proportions of the huge building which so attract the eye; nevertheless, I cannot wholly account for the impression it leaves on the mind, of a peculiar solemn magnificence that can never be understood until experienced. When first I caught sight of the Taj through the lofty gateway at the entrance to the grounds, I felt the strangest feelings of mingled awe and excitement, which only increased as I neared the building. The gardens in which it stands are very charming, there are white marble tanks of water, broad marble walks beneath shady trees, with seats here and there to rest the weary sight-seer. Sweet-scented flowers and shrubs, and the solemn funereal cypresses which abound in these gardens, set off the profusion of white marble, which is the chief feature in this lovely picture. The enormous platform on

E

which the Taj stands is white marble inlaid with precious stones, and the lower half of the outside of the building is most elaborately and tastefully inlaid in a somewhat similar manner. The variety of stones is very great, but among them I noticed amethysts, cornelians, blood stones, agates, lapis lazuli, jasper, &c., &c. The dome is plain white marble with a minaret of gold. There are apartments resembling cloisters, or inclosed verandahs, inside the building, and on the outside of the centre inner portion of it. Both are lit by windows of finely carved white marble, each window being a large slab several inches thick, and yet semi-opaque. In the centre, under the dome, is the show tomb of Mamtaz Mahal the favourite Queen of Shah-Jehan, to whose memory the Taj was built two centuries ago. She is interred in the crypt; and her real, as also her show tomb, above, is a mass of inlaid work. There is a wall built round the latter, composed entirely of the most splendid and the very finest mosaic work—lilies, leaves, and flowers of sorts, containing hundreds of precious stones. Each of one kind of lily is composed of between three and four hundred stones; and, when one thinks of the thousands of similar flowers in this stupendous edifice, one is lost in wonder as to how it was ever built; the enormous wealth, as well as art and care required, would, one would imagine, have been impracticable two hundred years ago. However, it was not so, and the great sight of the North-West of India remains a witness to the fact. There is a marvellous result of the peculiar formation of the interior of the dome, which I believe no writer has ever mentioned. I refer to the extraordinary reverberations. The echo of one's voice produced a sound—unlike anything earthly— absolutely impossible to imagine, or adequately describe. There is only one sound to which I can liken it, and that, of course, can only be imagined; it is the sound as of that "rushing mighty wind" which filled the house of prayer on the day of Pentecost. It is a sufficiently awe-inspiring sound in the daytime, but tenfold more so in the dead of night, when other noises are hushed, and when the darkness in the building is made visible by two or three dull lights, which only shed a pale glimmer over the scene. There are four very lofty minarets detached from the main building, and standing on the four corners of the marble platform of the Taj. These can be ascended from the inside, and the energetic climber is well repaid for his trouble by the view of Agra and its vicinity which awaits him. The tomb of Isman Dowlah ranks high among the many sights of interest in and about Agra; the gardens surrounding it are the *fac simile* of those of the Taj, only on a smaller scale. The tomb itself is quite unlike; except that it is white marble, and even more elaborately inlaid with precious stones than the King of Mausoleums; at any rate, it appears to be so, perhaps from its much reduced size. It, like the Taj, possesses a platform and corresponding minarets; and, even though fresh from the wonderful symmetry of Mamtaz Mahal's resting-place, one cannot but acknowledge that that of Isman Dowlah is one

of the most glorious pieces of workmanship possible
to see ; the open-work carving in white marble is
wonderfully fine, and looked very strikingly beautiful
as we saw it by the light of a most brilliant moon.
I was told the thing to "do" was to see the Agra
sights by moonlight as well as daylight, and I shall
never regret that delicious drive in the cool night
air, laden with sweet perfumes from a thousand
flowers, nor the beauty of the broad and lordly
Jumna, as we crossed it over the rough bridge
made of casks of iron, with logs of wood laid down
over them.

CHAPTER IV.

Agra and Futtehpore Sikree.

E again saw the Jumna that moonlight night from another point, the King's Gardens—truly a delightful spot to linger in, with badminton and croquet grounds, and a large house high up on the river's bank, used as a dâk bungalow, and frequented by those ailing in health, and requiring a change. The Fort of Agra, termed the " Key of Hindostan," is very large, and the lofty, massive walls appear immensely strong. After entering, the ground continues to rise until the Summun Boorj is reached, and a most fatiguing pull it is up that paved road, until one can rest in the apartments formerly inhabited by Lieutenant-Governor Colvin,

and where he died from over-exertion, both mental
and bodily, during the siege of 1857. Near these are
kept the Somnauth Gates; they are elaborately
carved, are rather large, and entirely composed of
sandal wood, but very much beaten about by time.
The palace must once have been very beautiful; it,
and the fort were built by Akbar, the greatest and
most powerful Emperor of India, upwards of three
hundred years. Among the chief objects of interest
is a very large slab of black marble on feet of the
same; this was used as a bandstand for the king's
musicians. It has a large crack across it, said to
have been caused supernaturally by the Bhurtpore
Rajah, who, contrary to custom and etiquette, put his
slippered foot upon it; and tradition says the stone
cracked and bled from the desecration. The guides go
so far as to show the supposed blood underneath the
stone. This Bhurtpore Rajah took the Fort in the
seventeenth century, and destroyed a good portion of
the palace, besides plucking out a vast quantity of
precious stones from the beautiful mosaic-work. The

ancient gilt chair in which the sovereign sat to ad-
minister justice, and the stone seat below it, formerly
occupied by the prime minister, in the *Dewan-i-aum*,
or Hall of Public Audience, are interesting objects.
Within sight of these lie the remains of Lieutenant-
Governor Colvin.   His monument is much concealed
by rank grass, which has been permitted to overrun
it, and the aspect of the place wears a sad appearance
of neglect.   I thought how painful it would be for
any friends of this victim of that terrible mutiny to
visit his resting-place and find it thus; I thought of
the sorrowing hands that had laid him down there,
and of the loving care which had raised the monument over him; and I felt sad at heart when I gazed
around and saw the forgotten, lonely, deserted appearance of the mournful spot.   There is a large and
handsome mosque inside the Fort, with a very
spacious court; it was, I believe, used as a barrack
during the mutiny, when for several months the
Agra garrison took refuge within the Fort, and there
is another mosque nearer the walls.   Right through a

large slab of open-worked carving is a large round shot mark, this is one of the memorials of a former siege; and, further on, there are more breaches, now filled up, caused by the same shot. Before closing my description of Agra, I wish to say a word for the Star Hotel, not by any means the best known, but in reality, from all accounts, the nicest. The landlord is a European and particularly civil, the charges extremely moderate, and food excellent; the Hotel is in a central position near the Post and Telegraph Offices and the Mall.

Futtehpore Sikree is situated twenty-three miles from Agra. With four good horses, the traveller reaches the entrance of these extraordinary ruins in three hours; but there a pair of strong horses are required, to drag the carriage up the ruggedly paved and steep incline, which almost continually ascends till the highest point of this once powerful fortress is reached. This immense mass of now grand and beautiful ruins, occupying an area of many miles, was built by the great Emperor Akbar; they took twelve

F

years building, and were completed in the year 1571. The walls of this enormous fortress only extended on three sides, the fourth being walled in most effectually by water, which had been cleverly banked up for the purpose. The present walls extend for six miles, and there is still a quantity of water on the unwalled side, but nothing like in volume what it was in former days. It is now two hundred years since Futtehpore Sikree was deserted, and yet in many parts the buildings appear so fresh, and the corners of the stones are so sharply defined, that you could easily imagine that they had been inhabited during the last year. Some, of course, are quite ruinous, and the great Elephant Gate and others have completely fallen down, heaps of dust and rubbish alone remaining to mark the spots where once they stood. Soon after entering the fortress, you pass the ruins of Akbar's mint, the quarters of his body guard, the public offices, and other buildings too numerous to mention. After passing through the second gate, you arrive at the *Muchee Bowan*, a sort of Durbar

Court, and *Dewani-i-aum*, or Hall of Public Audience, where Akbar received the numerous princes and nobles who were under his sway, and who came from time to time to do homage to their conqueror. Beyond that is an open space with a tank in the centre, bounded on one side by a building which formerly was the chief Dufteri's or Clerk's Office, and is now converted into a dâk bungalow; it possesses a very extensive view over the walls far away into the distance. Two other buildings have also been fitted up for the same purpose; the largest was formerly the residence of the prime minister, and is elaborately carved and ornamented. Lord Northbrook spent some days there, and when H. R. H. the Duke of Edinburgh visited Futtehpore Sikree he stayed in this building. The third dâk bungalow was once the house of Miriam, Akbar's Christian wife; even now the frescoes are quite distinctly visible, and the bath a few yards distant from the house is in fair repair.

There are so very many interesting buildings among these ruins, that in a sketch like this I have only space to mention those most worthy of notice. Before Futtehpore Sikree was built, in the centre of the present fortress, lived, in a cave, a hermit supposed to be a very holy man; he literally dwelt among wild beasts, as in those days the place was infested by tigers, and other wild animals. When he died, he was buried in, or close to, his cave, and it was there that Akbar first erected the beautiful tomb which I shall presently describe, and afterwards the Fort and its wonderful buildings around it. The celebrated tomb of this celebrated hermit is in the court-yard of the great Mosque belonging to the Fort. The outer gate of this Mosque is the highest in India, its dimensions are perfectly extraordinary, and the carving, &c., is very fine indeed; the height of the gateway is 120 feet, the court-yard of the Mosque measures in length 428 feet, and breadth 406 feet, while the splendid porticoes surrounding the court-yard are 50 feet in height. Imagine the effect of this! The tomb is the most perfect specimen of marble carving to be seen any-

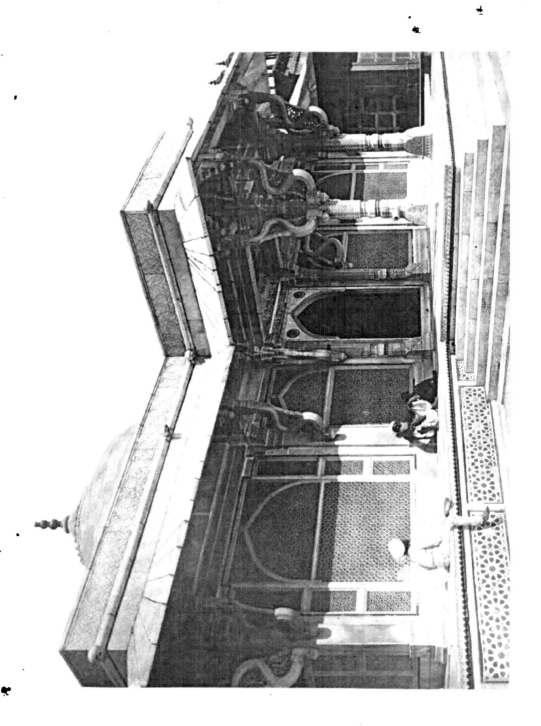

where in India. The first sight you catch of it
through the open gateway is very striking; it looks
as if made of the most beautiful carved ivory, and
at once reminded me of the ivory Chinese models
I had seen. The tomb is really, as I before said,
built of marble, and the entire outer walls are open-
worked carving, with other more solid ornamentation;
each slab of marble measures eight feet by six, and
is so fine a network, that I can liken it to nothing
but a very fine knitted anti-macassar, or Shetland
shawl; it is simply marvellous, and the lacework
of the Taj, in point of curiosity, is nothing to
compare with it. The flooring of this building is
very elaborately inlaid with precious stones; the
tomb itself and its surroundings are mother-o'-
pearl inlaid with silver; and, though it is hundreds
of years since the interment of this saint, the
greatest care is still taken of the place, and fresh
flowers are daily laid on the tomb. There are an
immense number of other tombs, all considered more
or less sacred ; the dead having been in some manner

related to the hermit.   Our guide also was a descend-
ant, and apparently took a great interest in showing
us everything.   The Royal stables are in wonderful
preservation; there are still holes in the corners of
the stones to which the horses were tethered.   The
staircases in the Emperor's portion of the palace
struck me as being the most uncivilized thing about
the place.   Imagine a staircase, almost perpendicular,
with a wall on either side, and steps at least 16 or
18 inches in height, and so shallow that it would
be a difficult matter to get either up or down them.

One of the best preserved and most interesting
buildings is the " Hide and Seek ; " this was built for
the numerous progeny of Akbar to play this ancient
and most popular game in.   It is a labyrinth of
rooms and narrow passages, with similar apartments
on the upper story, from which there is a fine view.
It is so massively built, that but for the handiwork
of the rebels of 1857, who dug up parts and removed
with tremendous labour some huge masses of stone,
in the hope of finding treasure, one might fancy that

it had been lately used by the little people for whose benefit it was built. The *Dewan-Khas*, or Hall of Private Audience, is a most curious chamber, in almost perfect preservation. In the centre of the room is a pillar about 15 feet high, upon which Akbar used to sit, from which run four bridges, each two feet broad, to the four corners of the building where sat the Ministers, these again being connected by a narrow ledge which runs round this rather perilous upper story; a false step on the part of Akbar or his Ministers would have precipitated them on the ground floor! The five-storied Palace or Panch Mahal, another great curiosity, was built as a sort of *Howa Khana* or place of airing; no part of the building is inclosed, and the structure is exceedingly massive, each story being supported by numerous stone pillars. The *Pucheesee* Court, and large block of marble on which the players—Akbar and his Minister—sat, is just as left by them. The usual way in which natives play this game is with stones, but Akbar employed women, who wore different coloured cloths, and stood, or sat, on the squares, which are still clearly defined. The vast ruins of Futtehpore Sikree are so full of beauty and interest, that, to see them alone, I am quite sure it would be worth any one's while to visit Northern India.

CHAPTER V.

DELHI AND ITS ENVIRONS.

THAT first sight of Delhi, the ancient city of the Moguls, can I ever forget? I had, for years, longed to visit the famous stronghold of the mutinies of 1857; and as the train ran rapidly within sight of the Jumna Musjid, then the river Jumna, the massive fort and palace walls, &c., all bathed in the early morning sunshine, my gratification and pleasure knew no bounds. I think that, without exception, Delhi is by far the most interesting spot connected with the mutinies, being so little altered—so much as it was just after the siege. The hotels in Delhi are very bad, the

G

best being the United Service; here we found an
excellent guide, who thoroughly understands his
business and is well up in the history of the siege,
&c. The eastern face of Delhi—the Palace side—
lies on the river Jumna, which, during the rains,
literally washes a portion of the walls. The river
is crossed by a fine railway bridge just outside
Delhi. The Jumna Musjid is the largest mosque
in the world, the next in size being that at Cairo.
There are forty steps up to the entrance-gate and
ground-floor, and one can imagine what a formid-
able obstacle was this lofty building during the
taking of Delhi. That Delhi was ever taken with
the mere handful of troops there were—between
three and four thousand—to sustain continual war-
fare for four months, at the most trying season of
the year, against a force of sixty thousand men and
upwards, is surprising. The strength of the walls
must have been very great; they are wonderfully
little injured considering all that they went through;
but still, of course, there are numerous breaches,

especially near the Cashmere Gate, rendered famous as long as the world shall last by some of the most glorious acts of bravery ever known. It was here, when Delhi was taken on the 14th of September, 1857, that Lieutenant Home with Sergeants John Smith and Carmichael, and Havildar Madhoo, all belonging to the Sappers, ran in broad daylight, with gunpowder bags in their hands, to lay the powder which was to blow up the Cashmere Gate. Close behind them followed Lieutenant Salkeld, Corporal Burgess, and others of the firing party. All were exposed to the most galling fire throughout the entire process; the wicket gate was open, and through it an incessant fire was poured upon the brave soldiers, of whom five out of seven fell. Salkeld was mortally wounded while endeavouring to ignite the train laid by Sergeant Carmichael, who was killed in the act. Though desperately wounded, gallant Salkeld handed over the slow-match to Corporal Burgess, who, having completed his noble work, fell also mortally wounded by the side of his officer. It was here that Bugler Hawthorne, after having three times repeated the signal call for the advance of the column, devoted himself to binding up the wounds and otherwise caring for Salkeld. This, and the removal of the wounded officer, he accomplished under the most terrible fire, utterly regardless of his own imminent danger. I was told at Delhi that the rebels were so astonished at the excessive intrepidity of this blowing up of the Cashmere Gate that, for some minutes, they slackened fire from sheer amazement at the bravery of the attempt. To thoroughly appreciate this heroic deed one must visit the spot. The road down which these brave men had to pass was immediately under the fire of two batteries, besides being exposed to a storm of round shot and bullets from other more distant parts of the walls. The hole in which the powder was placed, the ditch through, and the pathway up which the remains of the gallant band retreated, and the breaches through which the storming party—a company of Her Majesty's 52nd under the

command of Captain Bayley—rushed to victory, remain as memorials of some of England's finest and
best soldiers. At another part of the walls is a slab
showing the exact spot where that brave, lamented
officer, Brigadier-General Nicholson, while with up-
raised arm he was encouraging on his men, fell
mortally wounded. There is also a lane called
" Nicholson's lane," where, while being carried to
the rear, he expired. The remains of Nicholson
lie in a well-cared-for tomb in the pretty graveyard;
and most sacred will the spot ever be, as the resting-place of this noble officer, who was so beloved
and honoured by his men that, after his death, their
war-cry on going into action was "Remember Nicholson!"

The walls of Delhi are seven and a half miles in
circumference, and the Fort, which lies in the eastern
corner of the city, is three and a half miles round. It
was here that at the first outbreak Captain Douglas,
and several other European gentlemen and ladies, were
murdered; and it was within this Fort that the King

of Delhi lived. Seeing how beautiful the Palace now is, one can imagine how splendid it must have been before the rebels destroyed the peacock throne; the cost of which, being richly ornamented with diamonds, emeralds, &c., was £6,500,000. The Dewan Khas, or private audience chamber, in which it once stood, is a very handsome apartment; it is white marble inlaid with precious stones, and with a very handsome ceiling inlaid with gold. The rebels made away with several of the stones; and these have been replaced by composition, which is a poor substitute. The bathing rooms in the palace are the most charmingly cool retreats. In those marble palaces one scarcely feels the heat at all. The " Pearl Mosque " is very pretty, entirely white marble; it is one of the few buildings which remain as evidences of the former splendour of Delhi.

The Queen's Gardens are extremely well worth seeing; they are three miles in circumference, and the trees about them are very fine. A canal, which is a remarkably pretty object, completely shaded by overhanging trees, with pleasant paths on either side, runs through a part of the gardens; the roses there are, I think, extraordinary—the richest perfumes and most varied colours, while the clusters and marvellous profusion of them are something quite uncommon. The soft green lawns, the *parterres* of brilliant flowers, the drives, and, in short, everything in and about these beautiful gardens presents the greatest attraction to the tourist.

The Golden Mosque in the principal street of Delhi—the Chandni Chowk—is worthy of notice; as also the street itself, which is very broad, and is inhabited chiefly by jewellers, and shawl merchants. The Mosque is white marble with three golden minarets, and was built by Nadir Thah, or Kouli Khan in 1738, when he invaded Delhi, and when, in the open space near the Mosque, he caused 150,000 people to be massacred, and plunder was secured to the amount of £62,000,000 sterling. Similar horrors were undergone at Delhi in 1339, when the Mogul Tartars, under Tamerlane, invaded Hindostan; and again in 1751, when Abdulla, king of Candahar, invaded the country.

Ludlow Castle, the present residence of the Chief Commissioner, was well shelled during the siege, it being between the city and the Ridge occupied by the besiegers, and from which they originally drove the rebels, who had taken possession of it. The Ridge lies on the western side of Delhi, about two miles and a half distant from the city walls, and is the very last spur of the Aravelli Mountains, than which a better position could hardly be conceived for a besieging force, as it commands all the surrounding country for many miles; and the ravines, caused by the drainage from the Ridge on the east, afforded excellent protection for the troops. The besiegers' camp lay behind the Ridge, which is like a broad high embankment, on which there is now a road. From it can be seen the old Residency, which was partially burnt by the rebels soon after it was vacated by the fugitive ladies, who, during that fearful night, at the first outbreak of the troops, fled across country to the Ridge, and rested themselves as best they might in the " Flag Staff " tower, in front of which the main battery was afterwards placed. The poor ladies remained there in an agony of terror for an hour and a half, until they were enabled to escape, conveyances having been secured for them. One of their number remained with her husband all through those four trying months, and was the only lady who endured the hardships of the siege, during which she gave birth to a son. The " Flag Staff " tower is now just as it then was; and the impromptu walls here and there on the Ridge, hastily raised by the gunners, still remain. Hindoo Rao's house—the main picquet, and object of continual attack—which stands on one end of the Ridge, and which he presented to government, is now a hospital. Between it and the " Flag Staff " tower is an ancient pillar which dates from the third century before Christ; it is in wonderful preservation.

The memorial monument of the killed and murdered during these dreadful months at Delhi

H

is erected on the Ridge ; it can be seen for miles in all directions, but is decidedly ugly.

The little mosque is still standing up to which, on one occasion during the siege, the rebels approached ; it is only a short distance from the Ridge, so they got well punished for their temerity, and had to retreat with considerable loss, carrying a large number of dead and wounded with them, and leaving some hundreds behind them in the ditch. The bright red walls of the Fort form a conspicuous object, and nearly the whole of the road to Delhi is visible from the Ridge. Near the outside of the Cashmere Gate is the flat-roofed house on the top of which, towards the end of the siege, the guns were placed that opened the breaches through which the final rush was made on that glorious 14th of September. The dâk bungalow gateway and compound are objects of much interest, as here stood the magazine which that brave and noble officer, Captain Willoughby, blew up at the commencement of the insurrection, so that it should not fall into the hands of the rebels. He was, of course, killed on the spot, and no man ever deliberately sacrificed himself for his country in a more gallant manner than did this fine soldier.

The city of Delhi, as it now stands, was built in the seventeenth century by Shah-Jehan, or, King of the World; but for forty miles outside the walls are ruins of former and more ancient Delhis in all stages of decay. As we drove along, we passed forts, mosques, tombs, gateways, and other buildings of various dimensions,—some in very fair preservation; and most of which must once have been beautiful. Our guide showed us a minaret over the gateway of an old mosque, in which the Emperor Humayoon was said to have been sitting, listening to the reading of the Koran in the mosque below, when he suddenly determined to descend, and, missing his footing, fell down the difficult staircase, and if it was anything like those previously described in my account of Futtehpore Sikree, it is little wonder that such a descent should have resulted in his

death.   He was interred in the huge mausoleum
which is now one of the sights of Delhi ; it is an
enormous height, and the lower portion of the building is literally full of the dead, it being a mass of
sepulchres.   In one, quite underneath the building,
and almost entirely dark, the King of Delhi is said
to have hidden when he escaped from Delhi on the
troops taking it.   It was here he gave himself up,
finding resistance impossible, to gallant Major Hodgson, who, while bringing his captive back to the city,
caught and shot in the King's presence his two sons,
Mirza Moghul and Mirza Kheye Sultan, also his
grandson, Mirza Aboo Bukker, all of whom had
sanctioned and abetted the atrocities committed
during the mutiny of the troops.

The sights of interest in old Delhi are so numerous, that I can only mention a few of them.   The
poet Khusaro's tomb, the author of the *Bagh-o-Bahar*,
is a most sacred spot, and is a fine specimen of
the Agra marble-carving ; there are other tombs of
princes and princesses, one of the latter being a

poetess, all surrounded by walls of open-worked carving. Near these tombs is a deep and spacious well of water, which is the scene of a most extra-ordinary exploit; into this, from a height of seventy-five feet, numerous men and boys spring, disappear, and after a few seconds rise to the surface, and swim off to the steps to remount the height, and go through the same feat again. At first it was a most unpleasant one to witness, as it appeared impossible that this perfect shower of human beings, could all avoid striking against the rocks, or walls of the well; but long practice has taught them to exactly measure their distance, and they gain a livelihood by performing in this manner, for the benefit of every visitor to the ruins. The Kutub Minar is eleven miles from Delhi; it is an extremely lofty and ancient pillar, from the top of which there is a fine view of the interesting and picturesque country, surrounding the ruins of bygone Delhis, and of the present long-suffering survivor.

CHAPTER VI.

LUCKNOW.

ALTHOUGH Lucknow possesses nothing half so fine in the way of buildings as either Agra or Delhi, yet it is one of the most interesting spots in India. Our first drive through the place was sufficient to make us realize that we were visiting the scene of some dreadful conflict. Graves and tombs of the murdered and slain are to be seen at almost every turn, till at last one feels that the place is an enormous graveyard; and the sensations experienced are depressing. The sight which surpasses all others in interest is the Residency, which was the scene of the bravest and most determined defence in the annals of war. At the time the resistance first commenced the defences even were not completed; and from the 29th of June to the 25th of September 1857, when the garrison were first relieved by Havelock and Outram, every European had, night and day, to be on duty, and all had to lend a hand in building, repairing breaches, burying the dead, and other " fatigue duties." The assailants took up their position sufficiently near for the gallant defenders to hear their jeers and taunts, and they made good use of this proximity, and frequently for hours together kept the whole of that hard-worked little garrison on the alert and in suspense, by sounding the advance and yelling as if about to attack in force, keeping up a heavy fire all the time. The mosques and houses which surrounded the Residency were loop-holed, and the galling fire therefrom did more fatal work than the enemy's big guns. It is supposed that at least 8,000 men fired daily into the Residency; while the besieged became so reduced in numbers that, after a time, there were not so many gunners as guns.

The remains of the Bailey Gate are well worth
seeing, and tell a tale of great endurance. The outer
gate and defences are entirely gone, but portions of
the walls, parapets, and numerous buildings remain
exactly as left by the rebels, who, after the retirement
of the troops, destroyed a good deal that was in fair
repair. The Residency grounds are most beautifully
kept; the scene of all this misery and bloodshed,
terror, and suspense is now a charming, peaceful
garden, rendered doubly picturesque by the ruins
which are so sacred to every British heart. Slabs
are erected in and outside the various buildings for
the edification of visitors; one points out the room
where the noble Sir Henry Lawrence was struck
down; another shows the apartment in which, after
two days of great agony, he expired. It is strange
that, on the day previous to that on which he was
mortally wounded, an 8-inch shell burst in the same
room—the one in which Sir Henry was sitting; his
friends begged him to change his abode, but he
remarked that it was next to impossible that another

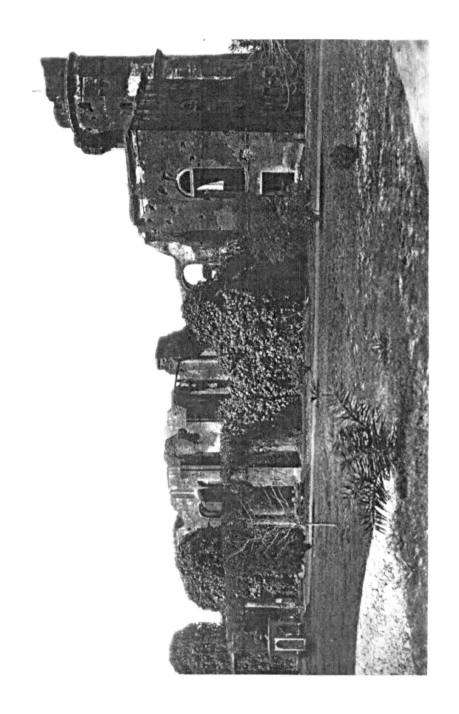

such missile would enter so small an apartment·
Another curious and disagreeable fact is, that the
shell which did this fatal work was fired from an
8-inch howitzer that fell into the rebels' hands at
Chinhut, just before the investment. This gun was
destined to do a great deal of damage to its rightful
owners, and helped considerably to batter the
Residency.

The well from which the beleaguered force drew
water is an object full of interest; beautiful creepers
now cover the trellis-work that shrouds it ; and
the remains of the Residency itself, where the
32nd Regiment and families lived, is in better preservation than most of the buildings. One can
imagine what a comparatively safe retreat these un-
derground cellars must have afforded to the women
and children ; for they lie completely under the house,
yet are not altogether dark, and can be approached by
two entrances. The once handsome banqueting hall
—now roofless—was converted into a hospital, and,
being near the Bailey Gate, was a constant object of

I

attack.　We saw the rooms, bathing rooms, che-
bootra (raised stone platform), &c., which had been
used by the ladies during the siege, many of whom,
having no servants, had to perform all menial offices
for themselves and their families ; and my heart
ached when I thought of the friends who had been
shut up there, and, later on, visited the graves of
those who had passed away during this time of
agonizing suspense.　The ruins of the Sikh quarters
that, on the 20th of July, were almost destroyed by
the explosion of a mine—one of the three successfully
carried out by the enemy—are still there.　Several
men were killed by this explosion, and three officers
were blown into the air, but came down unhurt.
The Fives' court, the pillars that mark the site of
" Gubbin's House" and other buildings, and the
Residency tower—the grand target for big guns—are
all objects of the most intense interest ; and last, not
least, is the graveyard where lie those who died, or
were killed, during those months of prolonged torture.
There rest Lawrence, and Neill, and Banks, and in

the centre of the Residency is erected the monument to the memory of the greatly beloved Lawrence.

The retirement from the Residency at the second relief was conducted in a most glorious manner. Havelock was in command, as it will be remembered that, after he reached Lucknow, he and his relieving army were, in their turn, shut up within the Residency walls from the 25th of September until the 22nd of November, when they got away in the middle of the night, and joined Sir Colin Campbell's force unknown to, though surrounded by, the enemy to the number of 50,000 men.

Right through what was formerly the inclosure of the Secunderbagh there is now a road, but on either side are the remains of the pretty gardens which, on the 16th of that month, were dyed with blood, when they were stormed by the 93rd Highlanders, 53rd Foot, 4th Punjab Infantry, and other troops, surprising the mutineers while cooking their food, and cutting down upwards of 2,000 within the walls. These gardens are surrounded by high loop-holed walls, and possess a powerful gateway, which is covered with shot marks. Its battered condition, and also that of the walls, attest the struggle which preceded the taking of Secunderbagh. Beyond the walls, at a distance of about a hundred yards, was a village also defended by the rebels. The breaches through which the storming party rushed are there untouched; and there, I trust, they will remain, to prove what poor defences are even well-armed walls against English pluck and valour. After this followed the taking of the Shah Nujjeep; both of these actions preceded the final relief of Lucknow under Sir Colin Campbell, and were brilliant successes. The Shah Nujjeep is a tomb; the inside and the marble flooring are very handsome; there are also innumerable gold and silver lamps, which are lit once a year during ten consecutive nights of a festival. The domed building is surrounded by a narrow court-yard, and that again by a garden inclosed by high loop-holed walls. Here a tremendous resistance was made; but, after three hours' heavy cannonading, the matter was settled by the gallant Sir William Peel, V. C., R. N., who brought his guns up close to the walls and battered them down in the most hardy manner. After this, the 93rd Highlanders, under the command of Sir Hope Grant, finally took the place; and I was told that 1,000 rebels fell within the inclosure. The Hoosseinee Bagh is a similar tomb, full of beautiful lamps; and here is to be seen a great curiosity—a carved solid silver staircase, on the steps of which the priests seat themselves to read the Koran. Within the precincts is an immense model of the Taj at Agra, but it does not convey the smallest idea of the beauty of the original. The marble court-yard and gateway of the Hoosseinee Bagh are very fine. The former contains a sacred tank, bridge, and boat. Not far from this is the " Muchhee Bhowan"—the fort which had to be relinquished at the first investment, owing to the paucity of defenders; had this step not been taken when it was, nothing could have saved the garrison. Dilkhoosha, which is now a handsome ruin surrounded by a garden with a bandstand, was the head-quarters of Sir Colin Campbell. It was here that Havelock died, and here, as elsewhere, are the graves of numerous brave soldiers. The Chutter Munzil Palace, the Martinière College, built by a Frenchman, Major Hodgson's tomb, the tombs of the first king and queen of Oude, the memorial of the killed in 1857, the Kaiserbagh, &c., are all among the sights of Lucknow. The gateways of the Kaiserbagh, which suffered a good deal during the siege, and the gardens, and palace, where formerly lived the king's women, are very handsome, but entirely different to those in the North-West Provinces. The Wingfield Park is very pretty, of considerable size, with fine old trees, and, like all the gardens in Northern India, is well kept. The Alumbagh—Havelock's head-quarters after the first relief—is his last home on earth. There are many graves near his, and though all are tended with the greatest care, and roses grow among them, yet the spot has a dreary look. Havelock's tomb is protected

by railings, so one can only stand outside and read the mournful tale so touchingly told.

There is a gateway in Lucknow which, though nothing to look at beyond the monument of a general surmounting it, possesses the greatest attraction for all true Madrasees; that is Neill's gate—in front of which the brave and intrepid Brigadier-General Neill, of the Madras Fusiliers, fell. The Motee Mahal—for several days his head-quarters—will also ever be to those of his own Presidency an object of special interest. It was within this inclosure that the elephant fights of former days used to take place.

CHAPTER VII.

CAWNPORE.

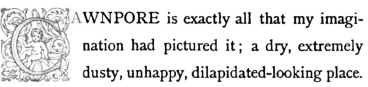AWNPORE is exactly all that my imagination had pictured it; a dry, extremely dusty, unhappy, dilapidated-looking place. Numerous fine houses, which formerly belonged to rich natives, are now fast crumbling to decay, having been deserted ever since they were hastily vacated by their inmates, on the arrival of the avenging troops during the mutinies of 1857. Most of the owners were killed, or fled never to return. Endless mounds of earth and portions of buildings are visible in various directions; and some represent whole villages burnt or destroyed at that time. There is something peculiarly depressing about Cawnpore. One wonders

how anybody can be glad or enjoy life there, for the terrible associations of the place must be ever present to the mind ; and, even if one could forget, the graves, as in Lucknow, of the murdered and slain are constant reminders. The station is ill-kept and untidy in appearance ; the best houses belonging to the residents are situated on the banks of the Ganges, which is indeed a lordly river. It is crossed by a temporary bridge to reach the station on the Lucknow Railway line, and it is then one sees the enormous width of the river at its height. The soil on either side is most peculiar, of a light-grey clay colour, and extends for a great distance inland on the Lucknow side, producing a strange weird appearance.

The objects of interest in Cawnpore are all connected with that fearful story, which can never be forgotten, and on which it is too painful to dwell : but a few words explanatory of the principal events that took place during that awful time may be acceptable to those who do not clearly remember them.

K

It was on the 6th of June, 1857, that the entire garrison of Cawnpore, with camp followers and most of the European inhabitants, retired into the ill-chosen and ill-fated intrenchment; where they were penned up until the 27th of June, without shelter or protection during the hottest season of the year. General Sir Hugh Massy Wheeler was then in command of the station, and had he selected the arsenal or some other suitable position, instead of the untenable one he chose, all might have been well: but as it was, being situated in a plain, the monsoon or rains which were expected at the end of June must, under any circumstances, have washed away the defences, and it was only three days after they were surrendered and vacated that the first burst of the south-west monsoon commenced.

All signs of the intrenchment have long ago disappeared, but the exact site of its centre, where stood the cavalry hospital, is marked by the Memorial Church, a very beautiful building filled with tablets to the memory of those who fell during those weeks

of direst woe in 1857. The cavalry hospital buildings were before the mutiny merely thatched, but when preparations for a siege began, in order to protect them from fire, they were hastily tiled in; these precautions however proved futile, for just a week after the commencement of the investment they were fired by the enemy and entirely destroyed, thereby depriving the sick, and unhappy women and children, of the small shelter they previously had, and also causing the helpless wounded to be burnt to death; as, owing to a strong wind blowing at the time, the fire spread rapidly, and a great number perished in the flames, and nearly all the surgical instruments and medicines were destroyed; consequently the sick and wounded from that time fared worse than ever, as treatment was impossible, and their sufferings must have been frightful. Added to all this, small-pox broke out among the besieged, and owing to the live stock being continually shot down food became scarce; *dhall* and *chupatties* (sort of cakes) doled out in small quantities were all that they had to depend upon.

Is it, then, to be wondered at that when Mrs. Jacobi, a prisoner taken and kept by Nana Sahib, was sent by him to the intrenchment with the false and treacherous offer of a " safe passage to Allahabad," that poor old Sir Hugh Wheeler should with his council of war have decided, that it was better to accept the offer than remain until forced by the elements to abandon the intrenchment? This they well knew must take place in the course of a few days; so, brave as were the spirits of that gallant yet desperate little band, the undaunted Captain Moore being their leader, they thankfully accepted what they hoped were means of escape from certain death for the loved and tender ones they had to protect.

The barrack No. 2, outside the position, which was so gallantly defended by Lieutenant Mowbray Thomson of the 56th N. I., and sixteen men, still bears shot marks about its woodwork. There is the well, now filled with rubbish, from which the beleaguered force drew water—water too frequently paid for with the blood of the brave men who drew it,

as, night and day, that well was one of the enemy's
favourite targets. A few yards beyond is another
well, surrounded by graves, inclosed in a small
garden, securely railed in, and always kept locked.
This was the burial-ground during those three weeks,
when, every night, under the cover of darkness, the
besieged were enabled to bury their dead in and
around the well. The Suttee Chowra Ghaut, com-
monly called "Slaughter" or "Massacre" Ghaut, is
now just as it was on that day of horrors, the
27th June, when hundreds of our countrymen were
treacherously slain by round shot, bullets, fire, or
the sword on those landing steps, or in the Ganges.
As I before said, I cannot dwell on the sad history ;
but should any one desire to know more than I have
the heart to relate, Captain Mowbray Thomson's
" Story of Cawnpore," or G. O. Trevelyan's "Cawnpore," will afford all desired information. The Ghaut,
which is distant three hundred yards from the road,
is approached by a broad ravine which, in the dry
season, takes the form of a sort of double pathway;

the centre being broken ground washed away by the
violence of the stream in the rains.   As we trod those
paths in the early morning sunshine, our hearts
sickened at the thoughts of that despondent multi-
tude which had passed down it on just such another
morn to meet their death, when they had hoped—but
I think hardly expected—that they were to be permitted to go on their way to Allahabad.   There are
the steep stone steps which pass underneath the
pretty Fisherman's temple, overlooking the Ghaut, the
old *peepul* tree which overhangs it, the platform in
front of both, where stood that arch-fiend Tantia
Topee, who was the Nana's executive officer on the
bloody occasion.   All are now exactly as they then
were, and, to look at the peaceful, quiet spot, one can
hardly realize the scene which, a few years back, was
enacted there.   It was on those landing steps that
poor old Sir Hugh Wheeler met his death by a
sword-cut, just as he was in the act of getting out of
his palanquin, from which he fell prostrate into the
water.   It will doubtless be remembered that some

three or four boats were already filled, and had put out into the stream, and the embarkation was still proceeding when the fatal signal was given ; the guns concealed among the high grass opened fire on the boats, the boatmen, having just previously ignited the thatched roofs, sprang into the water and made for shore, while the work of massacre had begun on the landing steps, and all there was dire confusion and misery.

Truly, those were happiest who died the soonest, and thrice wretched were the surviving women and children who, by order of the Nana, were conducted back over the weary road they had that morning traversed, and were taken, numbers of them badly wounded, and most of them destitute of covering for their heads, under that scorching June's sun to the pavilion where the Nana was quartered. This pavilion was situated across the *maidan* or plain near the race-course, beyond the barracks which were in course of construction. The Nana, on seeing his victims, ordered them to be kept in an adjoining

house called Savada Hall ; two large rooms were
cleared and placed at their disposal in this house,
which must once have been a very handsome edifice.
The punkahs still hang there, though, like the entire
building, they are greatly dilapidated ; but the broad
and lofty flight of steps which grace the entrance
are in excellent preservation, and bestow a melan-
choly splendour on the deserted spot.   It was in this
house that the Greenway family, and the Nana's
innocent emissary—Mrs. Jacobi—who were afterwards murdered—were imprisoned during the siege ;
and from there the unhappy women and children
reserved from the Chowra Ghaut massacre were removed to their last abiding place on earth—a small
house containing two centre rooms, where 206 crea-
tures, chiefly ladies and children, were compelled to
huddle together as best they might during the fearful
heat of July.   The final removal took place, as history
tells, on the 1st July; they were then placed under
the charge of an infamous woman, the servant of the
Nana's reigning favourite : the Nana was staying at

this time in a hotel close to the house in which the ladies and children were confined, and the night orgies held in celebration of his bloody victories, and in honour of his new toy, added greatly to the misery of the unfortunate captives. Cholera and other fearful diseases broke out among them, and death came to the relief of many; several of the most tenderly nurtured ladies had to perform menial offices, such as grinding grain; still hope must have remained, could not wholly have fled, until the afternoon of the fatal 16th of July, when within a few yards of the windows of their dwelling Mr. Greenway, his two sons, one a lad of fourteen years of age, and two other gentlemen were brought out and shot.

Soon after this, and through the instrumentality of the woman fiend who had charge of them, four men, butchers and sweepers, one of them being the paramour of this woman, entered the house and consummated this shocking and heart-rending drama. The poor victims had but short notice of their approaching end, and appear to have made some slight resistance. Three women and three children were alive and able to speak on the morning of the 17th, when the process of throwing the living and the dead down into the dry well belonging to the house where they had been incarcerated commenced. That house of horrors is completely gone, not even a stone is left to mark the accursed spot; but, surrounding the well and its beautiful Angel of Mercy surmounting its original wall and the outer walls of the sacred inclosure, which is raised several feet from the ground, is a most beautiful garden, one of the prettiest possible to conceive. It is most exquisitely kept, with the richest parterres of flowers and well-watered green lawns, and when the centre portion of the garden is approached a complete chain of cypress-trees marks the commencement of the doubly sacred spot. Close to the well are numerous graves of those killed in action later on in 1857. These are beautifully kept with roses and other flowers growing among them. The Angel of Mercy, although a beautiful monument, always strikes me as being out of place and somewhat inconsistent, considering that, for long after Cawnpore was again in the hands of our troops, numbers of rebels daily paid the penalty of their crimes on the gibbet erected over the well, just where the Angel of Mercy now stands. One of the two soldiers who with Lieutenants Mowbray Thomson and Delafosse survived the massacre at Cawnpore, was afterwards placed for some time in charge of the well; the other poor fellow never recovered the sufferings he had endured, and expired about a month after the surrender of the garrison.

We visited the Nana's house, where he used to reside when he stayed in Cawnpore; the only pieces of furniture in it were two old palanquins and a very old thermantidote. The keepers of the house looked a thoroughly murderous set, and they seemed greatly alarmed at our saying the house belonged to the Nana; they stoutly denied the fact, and appeared entirely content when we left them in peace. Cawnpore is celebrated for its leather-work, which is very superior—the best of Indian make. The natives of Cawnpore, of all places, struck us as being the most respectful, not to say servile, in all India. This was particularly noticeable at the Suttee Chowra Ghaut. As soon as we made our appearance on the steps, a number of dhobies who were washing clothes on the stones were immediately ordered by their chief to stop their work, for fear that we might get splashed by the water ; similar actions were observable on other occasions, showing that the inhabitants of Cawnpore entertain thorough respect for, and fear of, the English.

CHAPTER VIII.

Allahabad and Nagpore.

THERE is not very much to see at Allahabad, and I thought less of what there really was, from having previously seen so much that is extremely interesting and beautiful. The monster hotel where every one stays is certainly one of the sights; it is generally called "Kellner's Hotel," and is decidedly first class, with an immensely large centre room admirably adapted for music. Unfortunately, however, this room is, during the night, converted into a sleeping apartment for apparently every native in the establishment; consequently those whose rooms are adjacent find little rest or quiet; sounds of various descriptions, and not of the most musical order, being too frequent to admit of sleep. Allahabad is certainly a very fine, imposing station, worthy of being, as it is, the capital of the North-West Provinces. The place appeared more English than most of those I had visited, and the numerous fine buildings, broad, well-made roads, and green hedges give it a flourishing, prosperous appearance; but I was told that in a short time the pretty green hedges would be dried up. The native city is immensely large and picturesque ; but the sight best worth seeing is the junction of the two great rivers, the Ganges and the Jumna. The breadth of "the meeting of the waters" is considerable, and the railway bridge across the Jumna is a very fine one. The fort, built by Akbar, is spacious and well kept, with nothing particularly interesting in it except a pillar, which is the *fac simile* of the one I before described, at Delhi. It dates from the third century before Christ, and is in excellent preservation, far better even than the one at Delhi; it is much covered with ancient writing, and promises yet to

last as long as the world does. The Khusroo
Gardens are fine, and possess a double interest, as
having been the head-quarters of the rebel army
during the struggle in 1857. The Company Bagh
is another large and pretty public garden with a bandstand in it. Here is to be seen a relic of the Mutiny,
the remains of a Musjid that was blown up by our
troops; the domed roof came off in the most extraordinary manner, almost entire; and the ruin presents a
most picturesque appearance. During our drive round
the place, we passed a mess house in which ten
officers had been murdered at the first outbreak of the
mutinies. It will be remembered that it was gallant
Neill, of the Madras Fusiliers, who retook Allahabad
from the insurgents after a week's hard fighting. He
commenced in earnest on the 12th July, having
arrived the previous evening with the first batch of
about forty odd men, and by the 19th all the place
was in his hands, and the district was cleared of
rebels. The scenery, as you pass along the Railway
line from Allahabad to Bhosawul is very pretty, with

ranges of hills on either side. The Puchmurree range, the Central Province sanitarium, is to be seen on the left, and extends for a long distance.

Nagpore, the capital of the Central Provinces, is reached by a special line from Bhosawul. Nagpore city was greatly improved by Sir Richard Temple, and owns a fine market and very pretty tank—the Jumma Taloo. There are numerous schools, but one of the largest and most thriving belongs to the Free Church of Scotland Mission. Seetabuldee is the name of the cantonment and civil station, where there is one regiment of Native Infantry, the Magazine, formerly called the Arsenal, and a company of a British regiment. It is also the head-quarters of the civil administration of the Central Provinces, and, of course, the residence of the Chief Commissioner and numerous civil officials. It is a badly kept station as compared with Allahabad, and is very different now to what it was during Sir Richard Temple's reign when everything was in apple-pie order. Some of the roads, which were then excellent, are now barely passable.

Seetabuldee Fort, in which the British Infantry are quartered, is situated on the summit of the higher of the two Seetabuldee Hills. From it is a beautiful view of the surrounding country; it was on and around these hills that the battle of Seetabuldee was fought in 1825, and some of the graves of those killed in that battle are to be seen half way up the steep road which leads to the Fort. Seetabuldee owns a very nice little museum in which are excellent Assembly rooms. The new City hospital is a most imposing edifice, and has only lately been finished. The Residency is a miserable building for its purpose, and lies in by no means a healthy part of Seetabuldee. For some weeks during the troublous times of 1857, it was made into a sort of fortress, into which flocked all the Europeans in the place. The mutineers of the Nagpore Irregular Cavalry were found out only just in time; they were surprised on private information

M

being given at ten o'clock at night on the 16th July, saddling their horses in their barracks at Taklee, for the purpose of riding down on the Residency and murdering all the Europeans.   The ring-leaders were seized and were afterwards hung on the hill, and their bodies thrown into the ditch below the Fort. The neighbourhood of Nagpore is celebrated for pretty Government gardens.   To begin with Seeta-buldee itself; there is the Maharaj Bagh, which is most tastefully laid out, and possesses some remark-ably fine bamboos and other ancient trees.   The modern portion of the garden is used as a nursery for young trees and plants; and several acres of ground are so employed.   The Telingkerry Gardens are extremely pretty, with quaint and picturesque Indian summer-houses in them; also small orna-mental tanks, beautiful flowering shrubs, &c.; and beyond the gardens a very fine spacious tank, which, however, large as it is, is not half the size of the Ambajirri tank, which extends for miles, and is a splendid sheet of water.   The Sonagoon Gardens are situated about six miles from Nagpore, and contain two bungalows, which are used as domiciles for those needing change of air. The Paldee Gardens, nine miles from Seetabuldee, are the favourite resort of picnicers and of the newly married. There is an upstair summer palace in the centre of the gardens with shady, pleasant walks amidst the latter, which render it an acceptable retreat; and the tank near the gardens is pretty and picturesque. The Shuk-kerdurrah Gardens, about three miles distant from the city, is the scene of the battle of Nagpore in 1817. The tops of some of the old trees still bear shot marks; and on the original site of the ancient palace, which was blown up during the battle, stands a bungalow used principally for picnics, and which, in former days was furnished for the benefit of visitors to those interesting gardens.

Kamptee, which is ten miles from Seetabuldee, is the military station, and is far prettier, though less interesting, than Seetabuldee. Kamptee is one of the most beautifully kept stations I have seen in India;

the roads are excellent, and it possesses the very largest masonry bridge in India, being only three yards less than a quarter of a mile in length, and a very elegant and yet massive bridge. The cost of it was ten lacs of rupees, or £100,000. It was originally built with the view of constructing, on one half of the roadway, a railroad that was to pass through Nagpore *en route* to Raipore, from which place a direct line to Calcutta could be formed. Whether this will ever be carried out is at present doubtful, but that such a line would be of the very greatest benefit and importance to India is an established fact.

The Temple Gardens, in which is a bandstand, are pretty, but certainly not so well kept as they might be. They will, doubtless, in course of time, when the trees have grown up, be better worth seeing than they now are ; but after those at Seetabuldee, and the numerous beautiful gardens we had seen in Northern India, the Kamptee gardens seemed poor. Kamptee is four miles in length from the end of the staff lines, where the

Kanhan bridge is situated, to the end of the artillery lines. There is a nice airy drive of five miles out of cantonments called Blogg's Drive, near which is the race course. One of the great places of resort, about twenty miles from Kamptee, is Ramteah Hill, on the summit of which stands a sacred Hindoo temple.

On the plateau, a little below this, is a very comfortable furnished bungalow, built from some of the materials of the numerous ruined little temples which were demolished by Sir Richard Temple. From this bungalow, and all along this range of horseshoe shaped hills, is the most glorious view. It is certainly one of the finest to be seen anywhere in the plains of India; several large and smaller tanks, or lakes, some beautifully wooded, blending water with the distant and nearer hills; huge jungles and *maidans*, or plains, make up a truly beautiful picture. The hill is ascended by four routes; the easiest being from the village, of Ambarrah, by a flight of 666 steps, some of which are extremely steep. There are numerous resting-places on the way up, and it may be imagined that the visitor is very frequently tempted to stop awhile and gaze on the ever-growing beauty of the scene below him.

THE END.

PRINTED BY WHITTINGHAM AND WILKINS,
TOOKS COURT, CHANCERY LANE.

CPSIA information can be obtained at www.ICGtesting.com
Printed in the USA
BVOW04s1122020315

389917BV00020B/363/P